Piano • Vocal • Guitar

Bob Seger
FACE THE PROMISE

ISBN-13: 978-1-4234-2275-4
ISBN-10: 1-4234-2275-9

HAL•LEONARD®
CORPORATION
7777 W. BLUEMOUND RD. P.O. BOX 13819 MILWAUKEE, WI 53213

Visit Hal Leonard Online at
www.halleonard.com

WRECK THIS HEART

Words and Music by
BOB SEGER

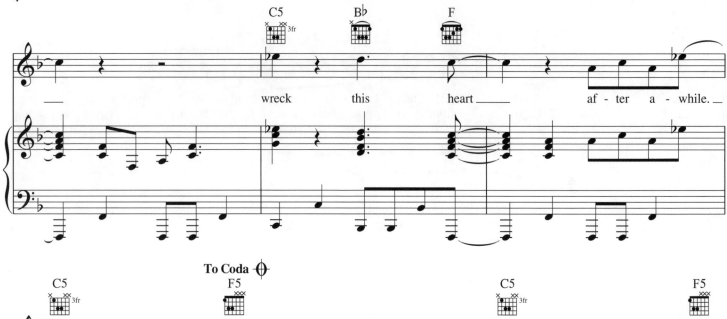

wreck this heart _____ af - ter a - while. _

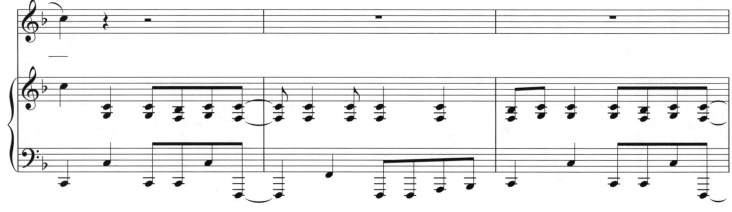

To Coda ⊕

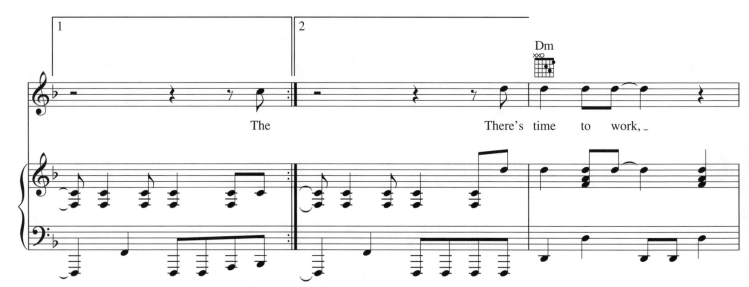

The

There's time to work, _

time to live, _ there's on - ly so much time _ a - round, _ and if you

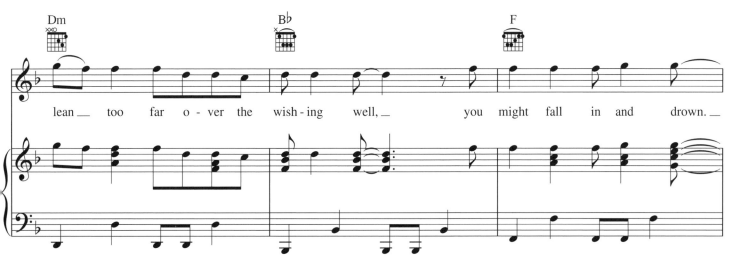

lean __ too far o - ver the wish - ing well, __ you might fall in and drown. __

Guitar solo

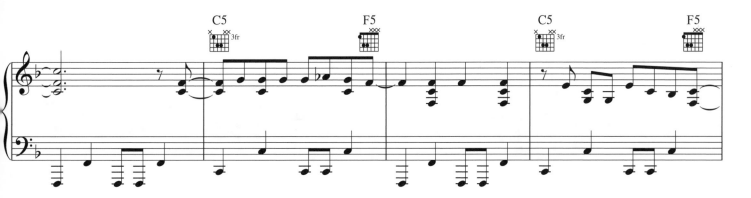

D.S. al Coda

Solo ends Am I

CODA

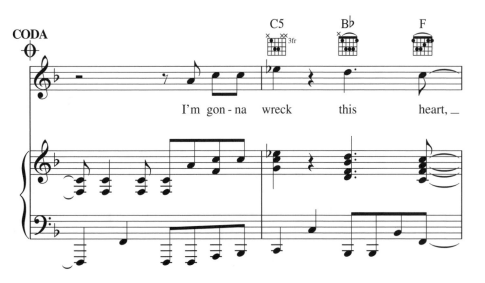

I'm gon - na wreck this heart, __

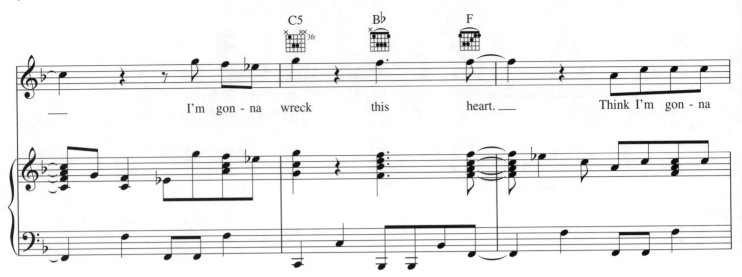

I'm gon-na wreck this heart. ___ Think I'm gon-na

wreck this heart ___ af-ter a - while. ___

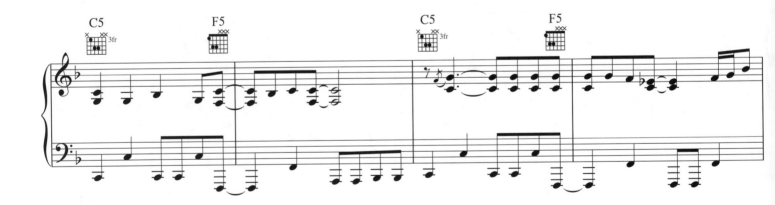

WAIT FOR ME

Words and Music by
BOB SEGER

Moderately

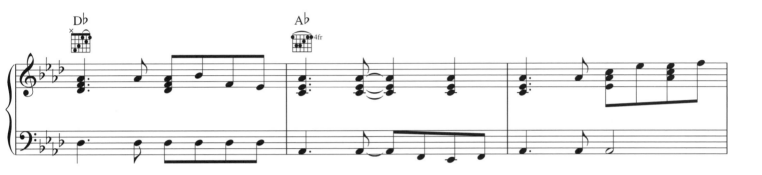

I will an - swer the wind.
rise.
night,

I will leave with the tide.
There'll be times when I'll fall.
in the heat of the day,

I'll be out on the
There'll be times when it's
if you're ev - er in

road .... ev - 'ry chance I can ride.
best .... to say noth - ing at all.
doubt, ... I'll be on my way

No mat - ter how far, ... no mat - ter how
Know - ing you're right, ... let - ting it
straight to your side, ... I guar - an -

free, ... I'll be a - long ....
be. .... I'll be a - round ....
tee. .... I'll be a - round ....

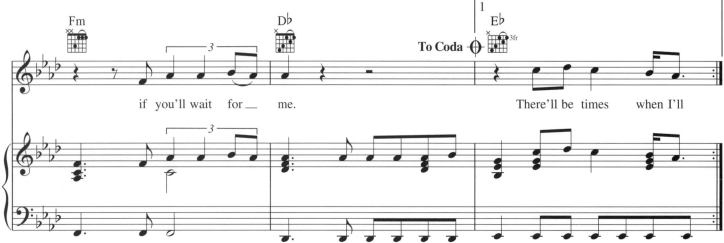

if you'll wait for __ me. .... There'll be times when I'll

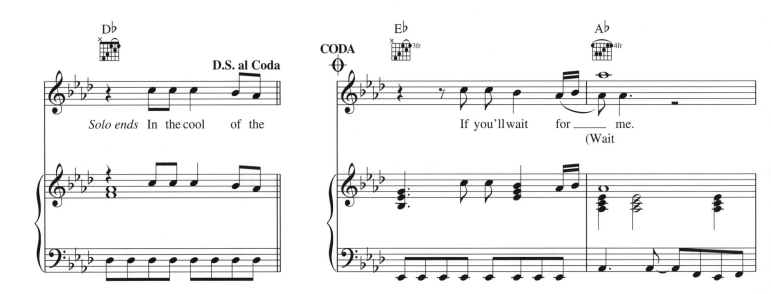

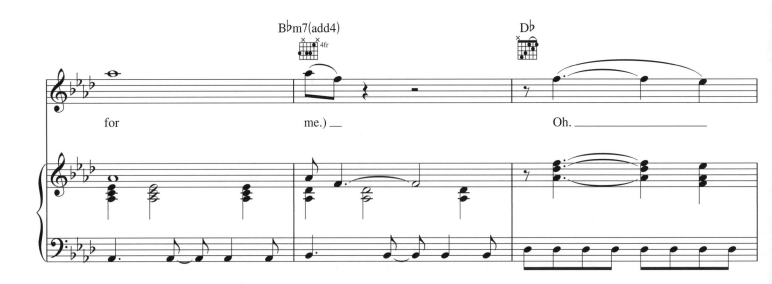

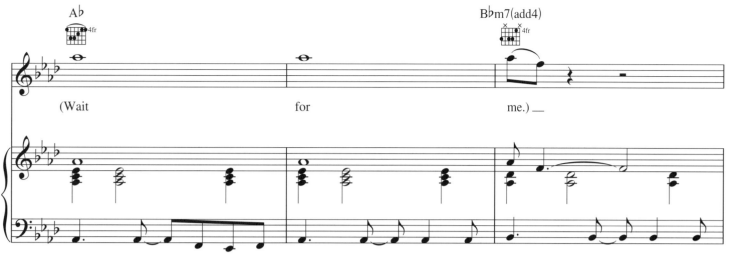

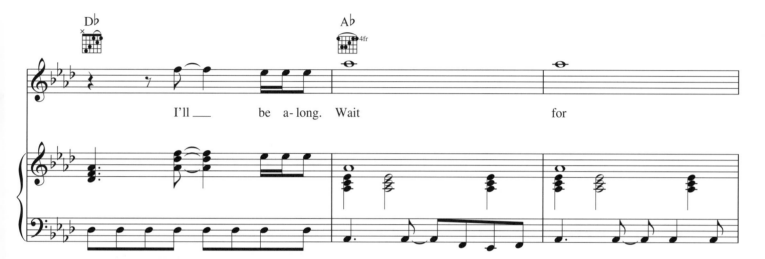

FACE THE PROMISE

Words and Music by
BOB SEGER

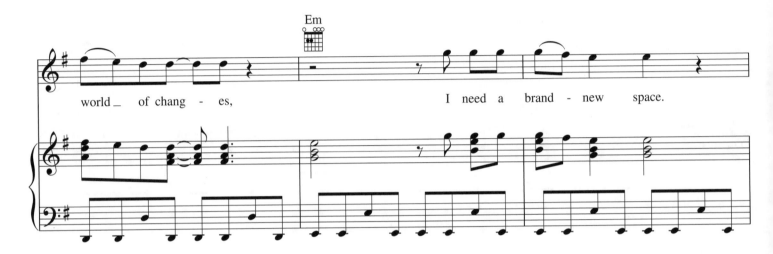

of the Prom-ised Land.

Em

(Face the prom - ise.)

8vb

Play 3 times

(Face the prom - ise.)

(8vb)

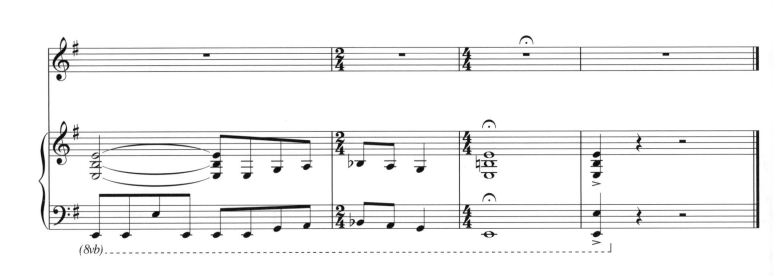

(8vb)

NO MATTER WHO YOU ARE

Words and Music by
BOB SEGER

yeah.
yeah.

This is an an-cient

No mat-ter who you

are,

no mat-ter where _ you've been,

no mat-ter what you've done,

you'll have to start _ a-

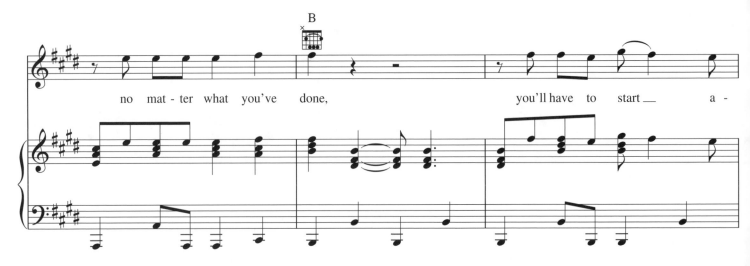

19

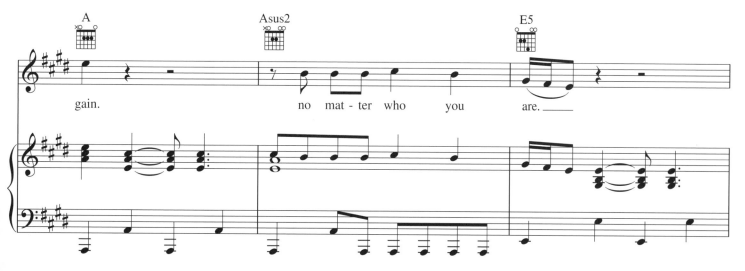

gain.   no mat - ter who you are. ____

Be - tween the soar - ing

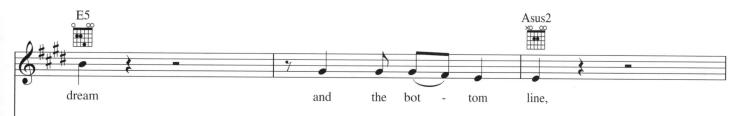

dream   and the bot - tom line,

so much is giv - en up,   so much is left ____ be -

hind, yeah.

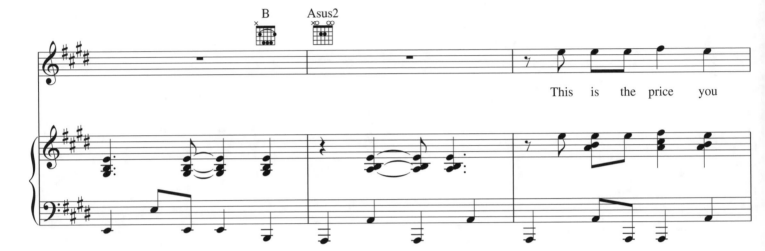

This is the price you

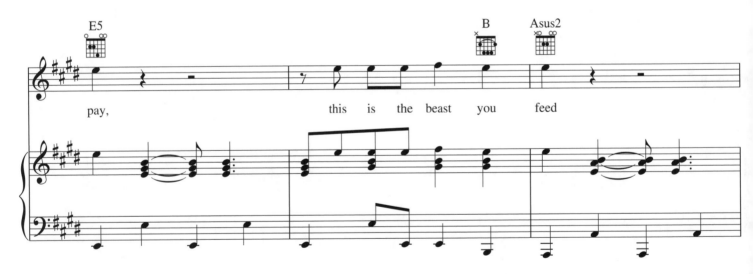

pay, this is the beast you feed

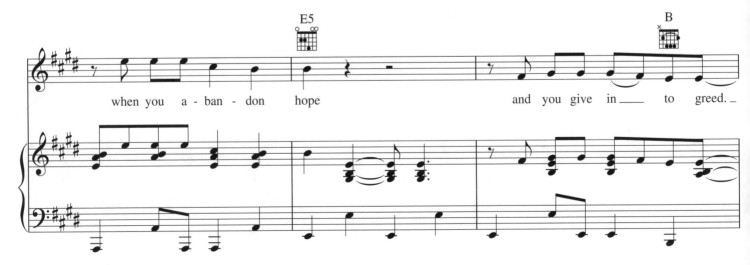

when you a-ban-don hope and you give in ___ to greed. ___

who _____ you are.) No mat-ter who you are. (No

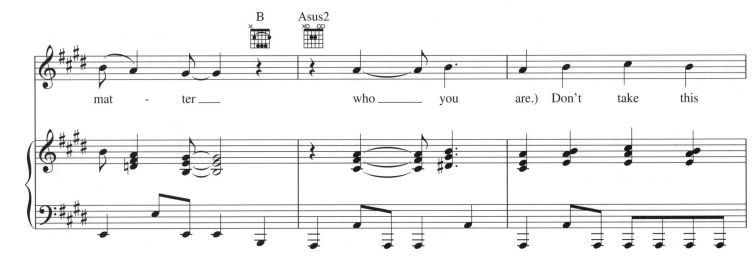

mat - ter ____ who _____ you are.) Don't take this

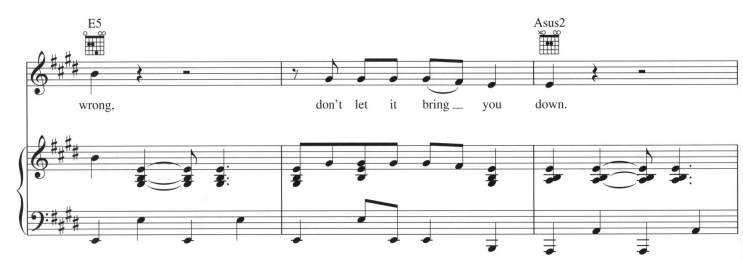

wrong, don't let it bring __ you down.

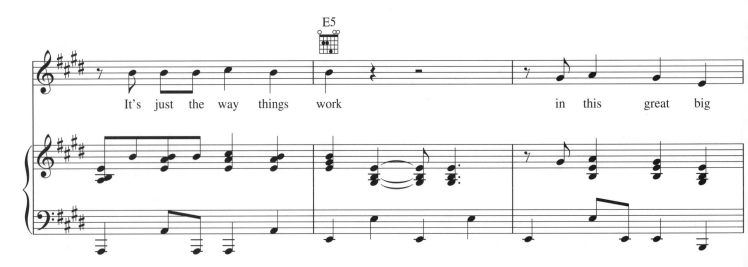

It's just the way things work in this great big

town,   yeah.   (No are.

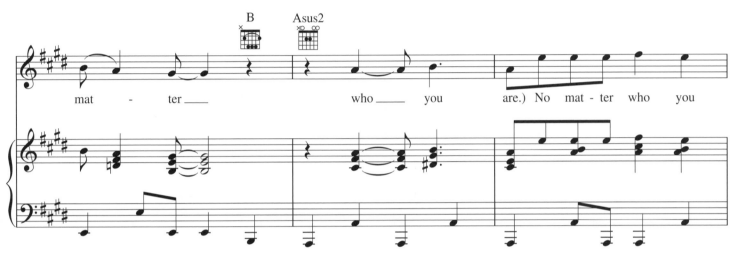

mat - ter ____ who ____ you are.) No mat - ter who you

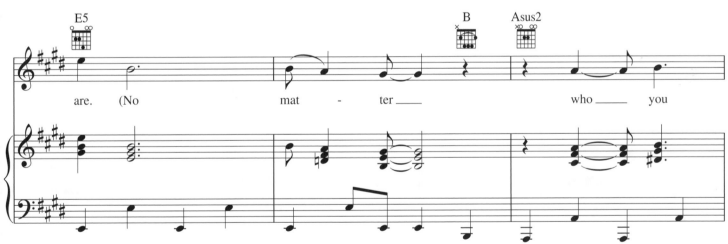

are. (No mat - ter ____ who ____ you

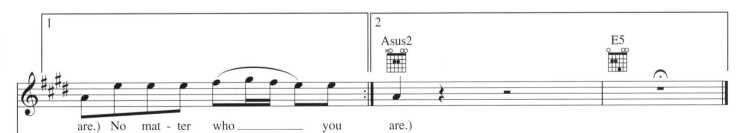

are.) No mat - ter who ____ you are.)

poco rit.

ARE YOU

Words and Music by
BOB SEGER

This is a whole _ new faith, al-most like a new _ re-li-

-gion. _ (Re-li - gion.) _ The lights _ are al - ways on,

the doors _ are nev-er locked. _ We ride in on the light, _ the shelves are o - ver - stocked.

Guitar solo

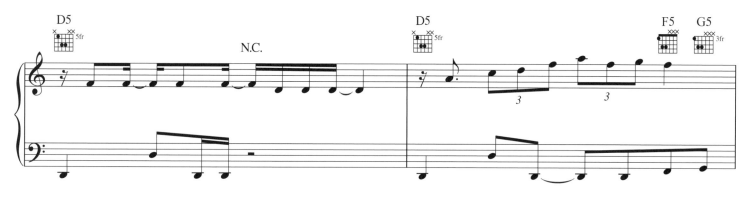

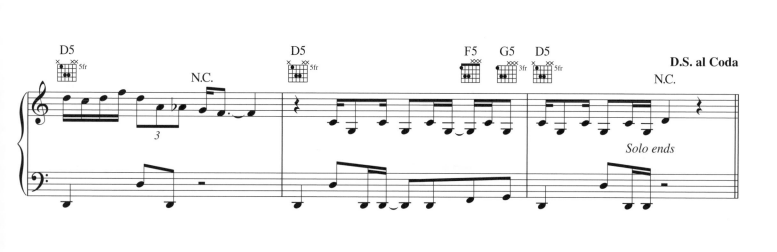

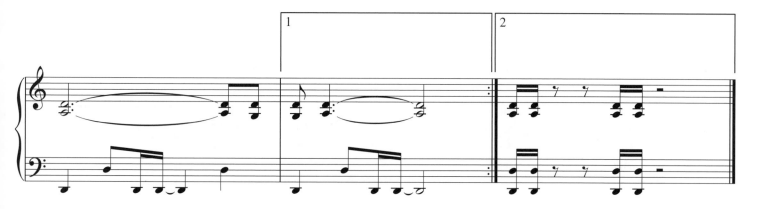

SIMPLICITY

Words and Music by
BOB SEGER

With a steady beat

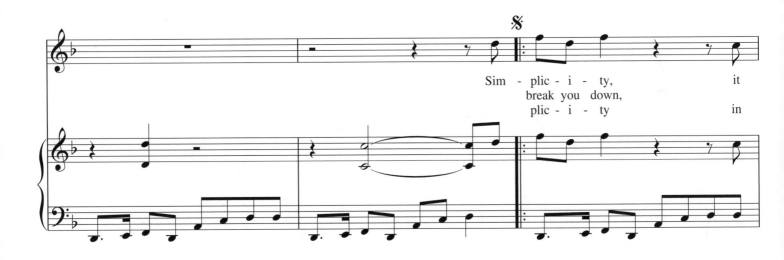

Sim - plic - i - ty,   it
break you down,
plic - i - ty   in

works for me.   It keeps me run - nin' hard ___ and sharp and
size you up.   I see a path ___ and then I bust a
ev - 'ry - thing,   in ev - 'ry sin - gle thing you say and

* Recorded a half step lower.

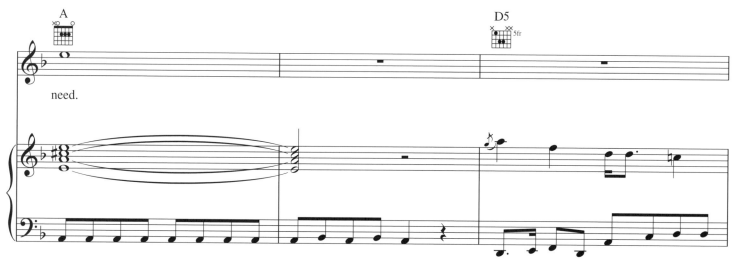

need.

D.S. al Coda

Sim -

CODA

Use your __ pow -

- er and your speed. ___

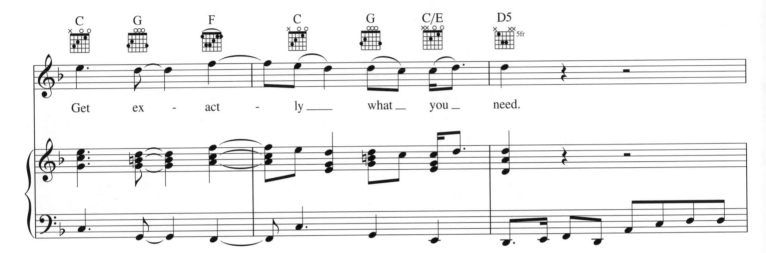

Get ex - act - ly ___ what ___ you ___ need.

Sim - plic - i - ty.

Sim -

NO MORE

Words and Music by
BOB SEGER

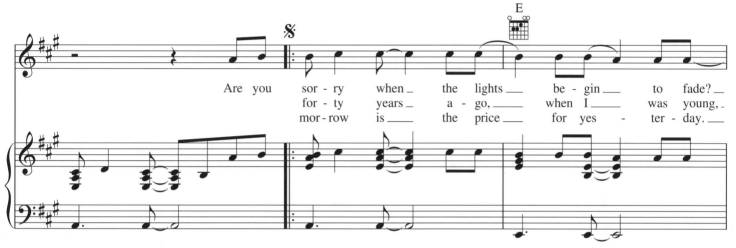

Are you sor-ry when _ the lights _ be-gin _ to fade? _
for-ty years _ a-go, _ when I _ was young, _
mor-row is _ the price _ for yes-ter-day. _

Are you sor-ry for _ the prom-
and the jun-gle, not _ the des-
A bil-lion waves _ won't wash _

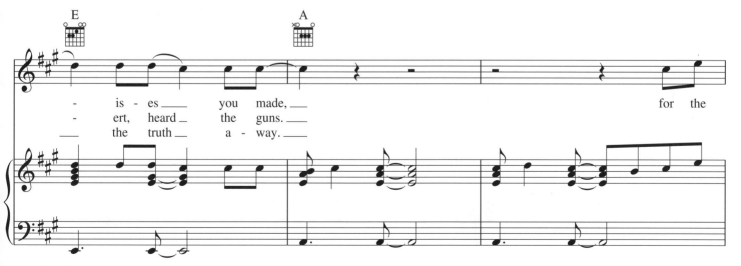

-is-es _ you made, _   for the
-ert, heard _ the guns. _
_ the truth _ a - way. _

bur - den of ____ the ones ____ who had ____ to fall, ____
Some - one said ___ they had ____ a se - cret plan, ___
Some - day you'll _ be or - dered to ___ ex - plain. ___

when you did - n't read ___ the writ - ing on ___ the wall?
and the rest of us ___ were told ___ to un - der - stand. __
No one gets ___ to walk ___ be - tween _ the rain. __

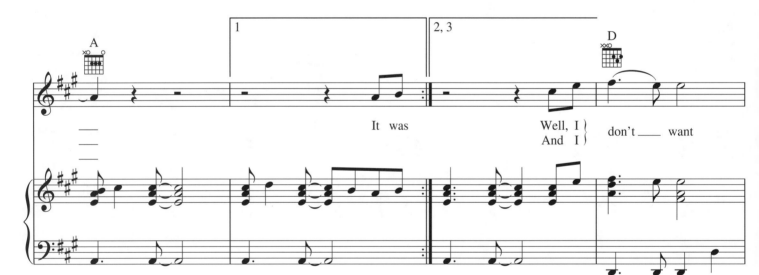

It was   Well, I
                And I   don't ___ want

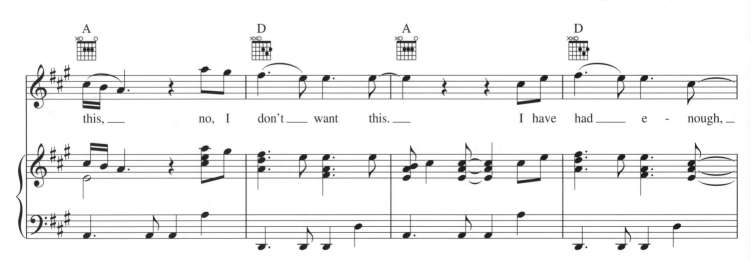

this, ___   no, I don't ___ want this. ___   I have had ___ e - nough, ___

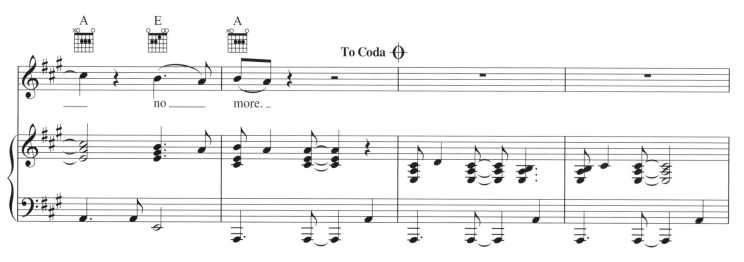

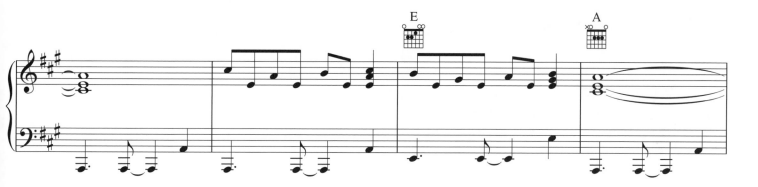

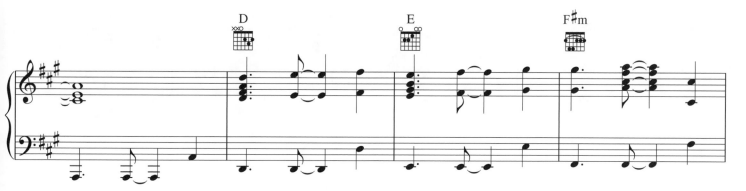

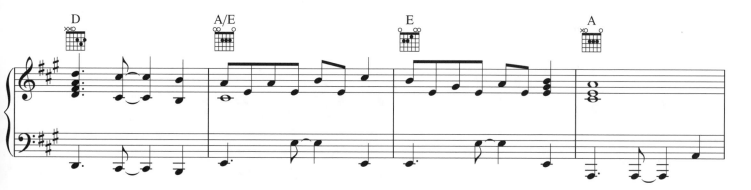

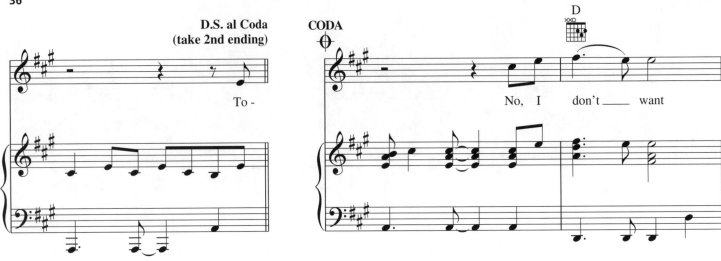

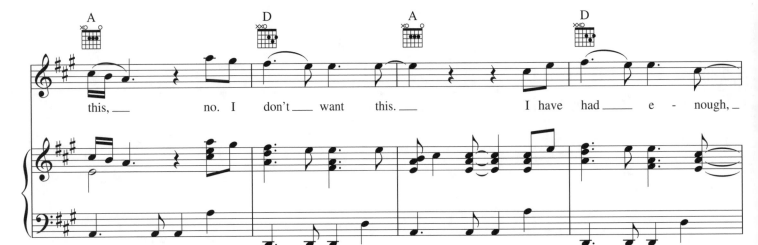

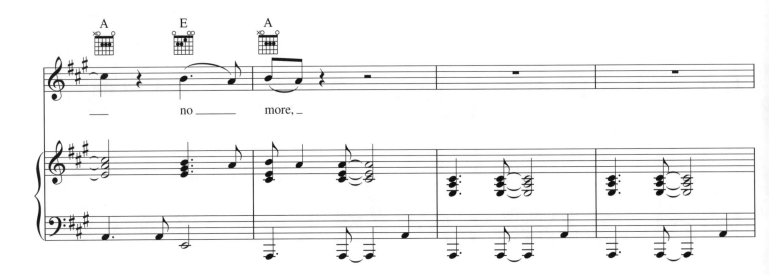

REAL MEAN BOTTLE

Words and Music by
VINCE GILL

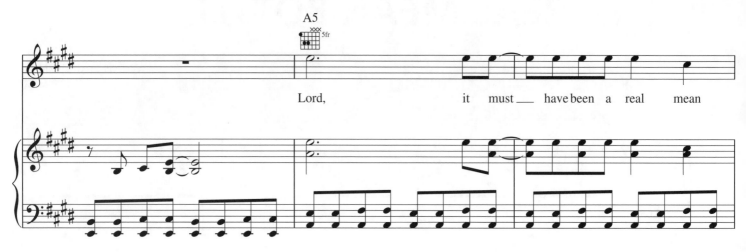

Lord, it must __ have been a real mean

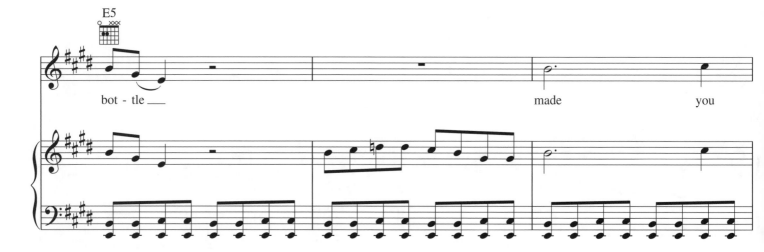

bot - tle __ made you

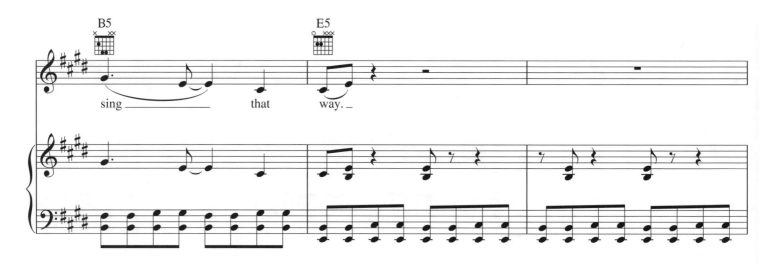

sing _____ that way. __

Sto - ries _____ you told a - bout pris - on, _____
spend _____ most all your life with stran - gers, _____

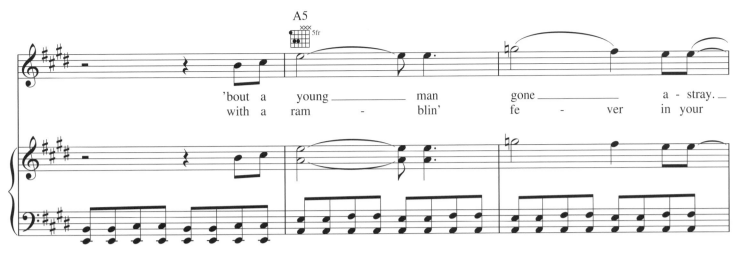

'bout a young _____ man gone _____ a - stray. _____
with a ram - blin' fe - ver in your

_____ veins. _____

Lord, it must _____
Hag, it must _____

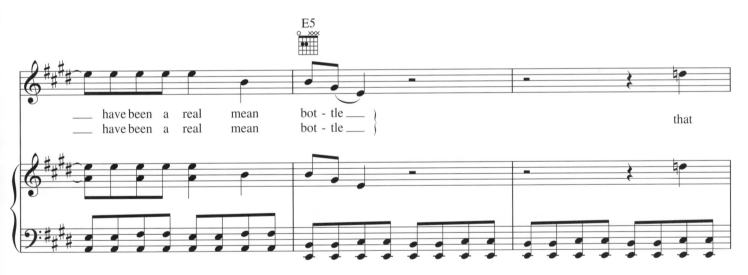

_____ have been a real mean bot - tle _____ }
_____ have been a real mean bot - tle _____ }

that

made you write the songs _____ that way.

A real mean bot - tle _____ poured

straight from the dev - il. And it's a mir - a - cle _____ that {you're}{we're}

stand - in' here _____ to - day. _____

A real mean bot - tle _____ made you such a

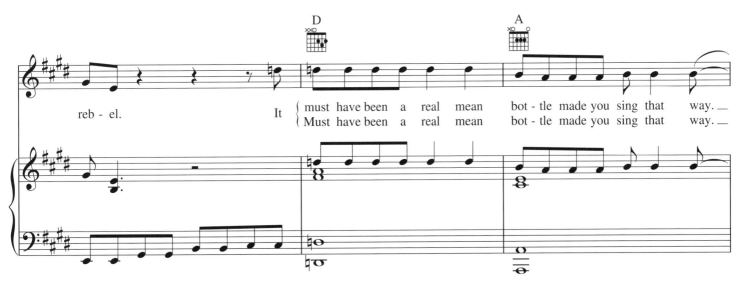

reb - el. It { must have been a real mean bot - tle made you sing that way. __
{ Must have been a real mean bot - tle made you sing that way. __

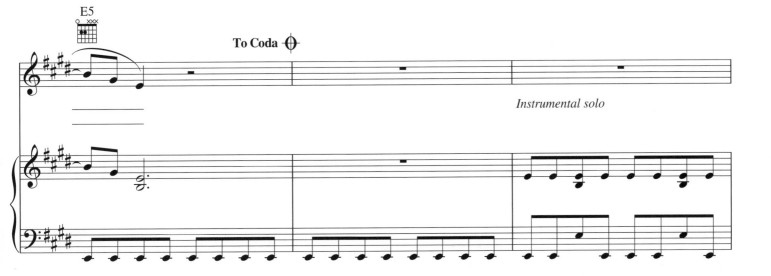

To Coda ⊕

Instrumental solo

D.S. al Coda

Solo ends   You

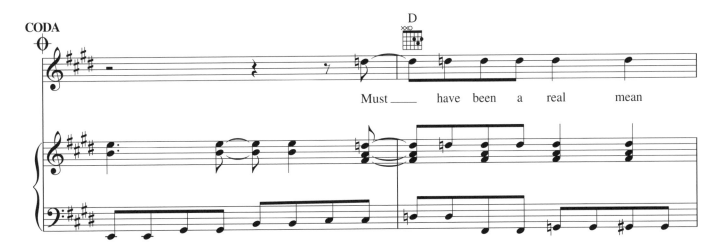

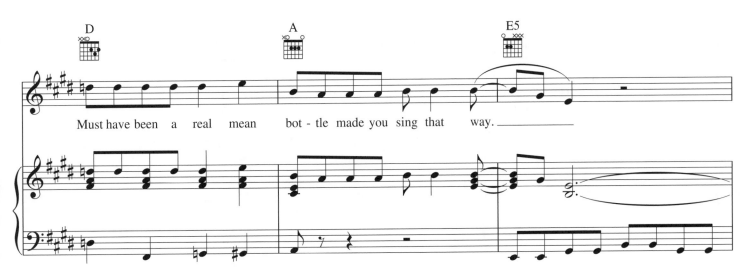

WON'T STOP

Words and Music by
BOB SEGER

With a lilt

You can

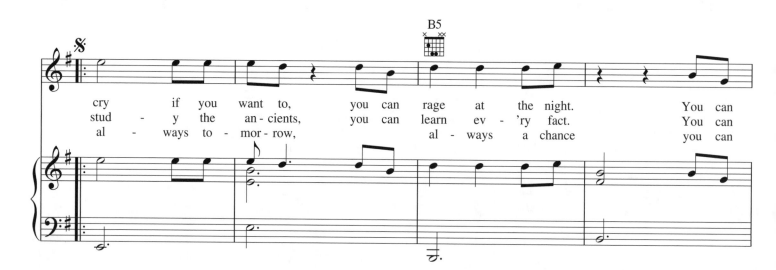

cry   if   you   want   to,   you   can   rage   at   the   night.   You   can
stud - y   the   an - cients,   you   can   learn   ev - 'ry   fact.   You   can
al - ways   to - mor - row,   al - ways   a   chance   you   can

blame   all   your __ wounds   on   the   world _____ if   you   like.   You   can
fol - low   the __ cy - cles   that   leave _____ and   come   back.   How __
stand _____ in   the   spot - light   and   not _____ have   to   dance.   You   can

won't ___ stop there.
won't ___ stop there.
won't ___ stop

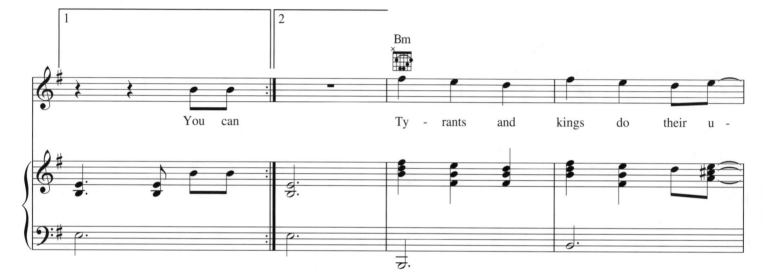

You can

Ty - rants and kings do their u -

- su - al things, ___ and you try to stay out of their

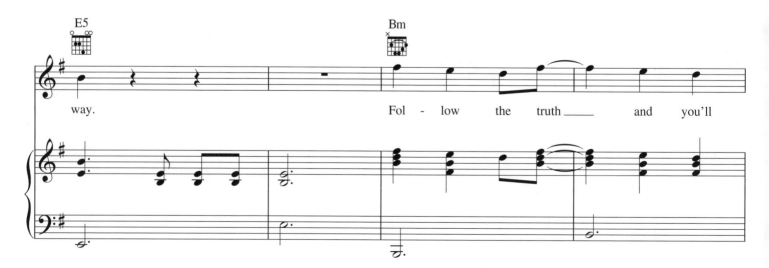

way.

Fol - low the truth ___ and you'll

find what you need ____ ev - 'ry day.

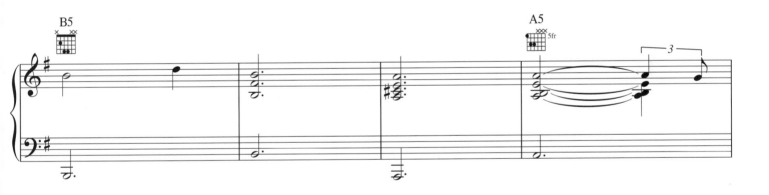

There's

D.S. al Coda

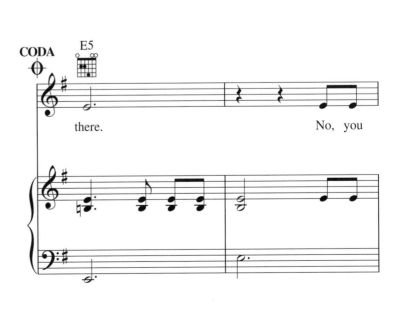

there.

CODA

No, you

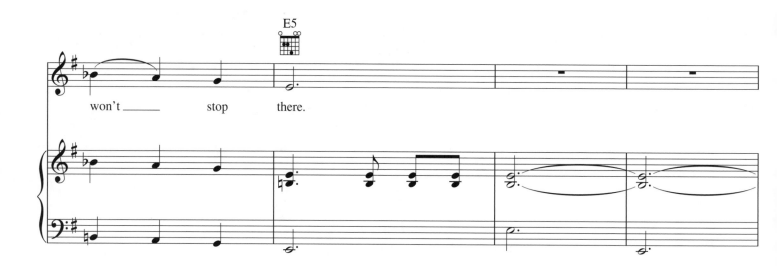

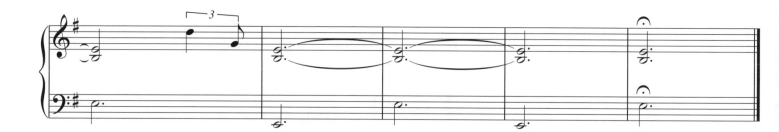

BETWEEN

Words and Music by
BOB SEGER

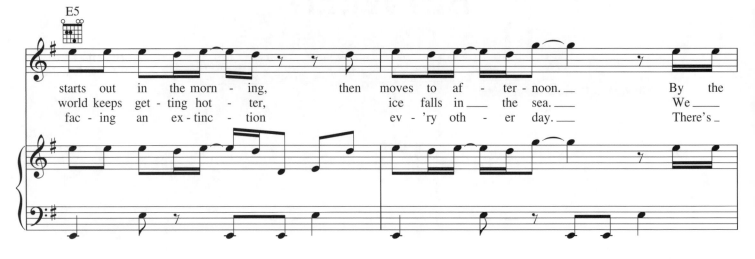

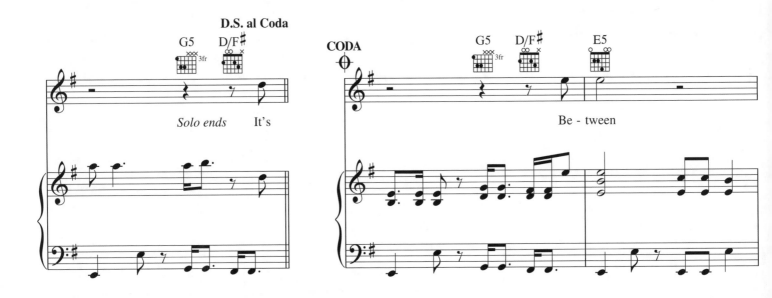

D.S. al Coda

Solo ends   It's

CODA

Be - tween

what is   fair __ and what's ob - scene,   it's

clean · far a-way _ from that ma - chine.

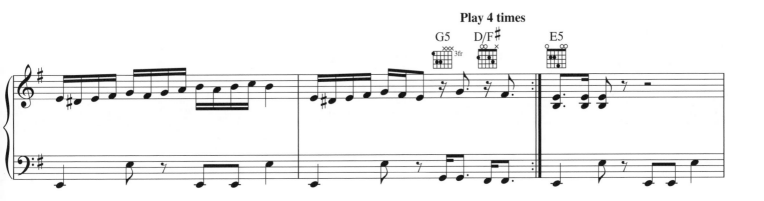

Play 4 times

8vb

THE ANSWER'S IN THE QUESTION

Words and Music by
BOB SEGER

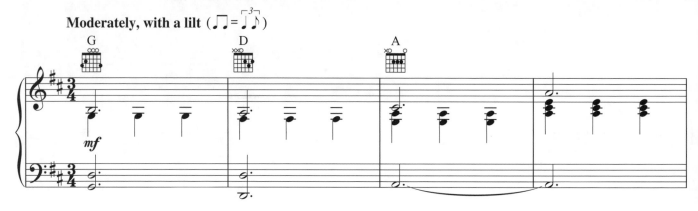

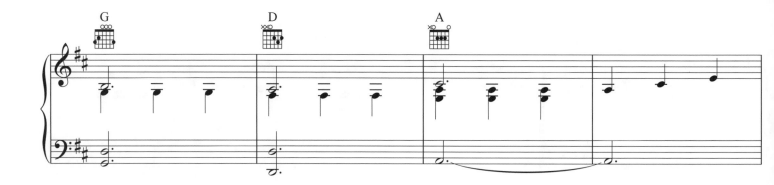

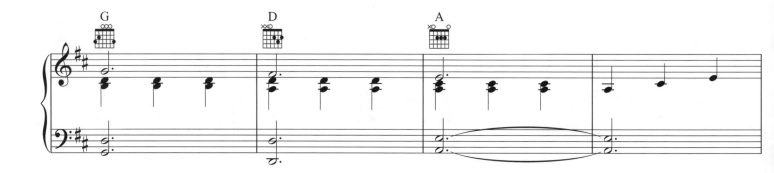

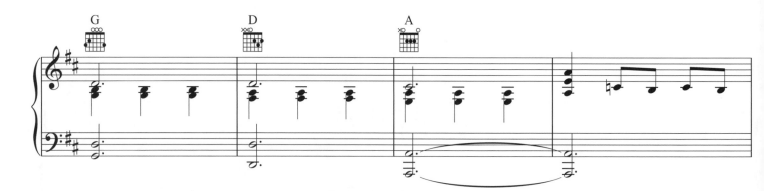

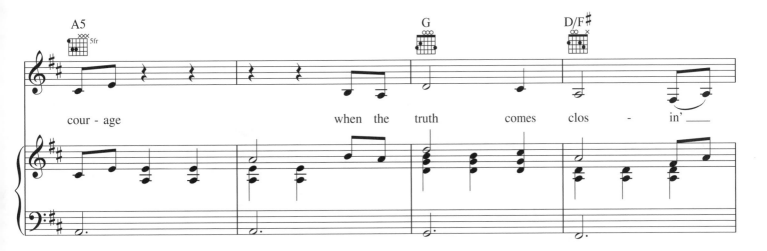

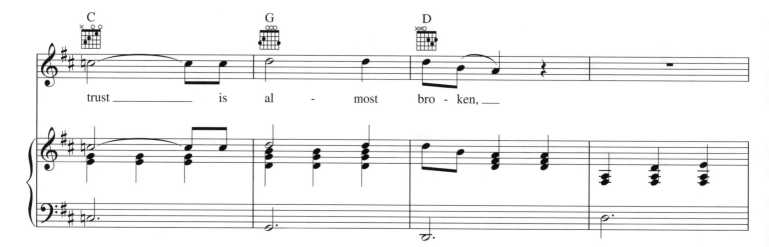

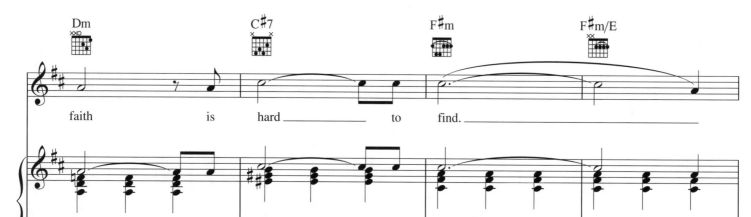

ques - tion.   Will you leave   this   all ____   be -

hind?   *Female:* The

heart's ____ a   lone - ly   hunt - er;   it

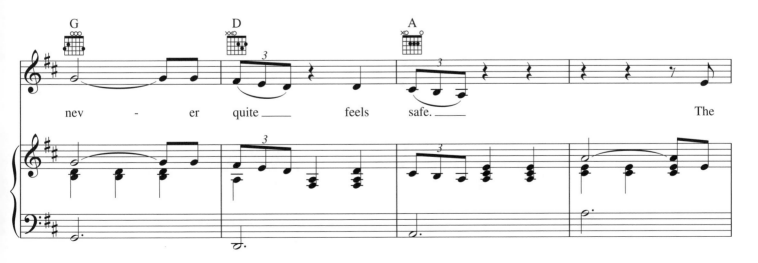

nev - er quite ____ feels   safe. ____   The

dev - il's in _____ the de - tails. The

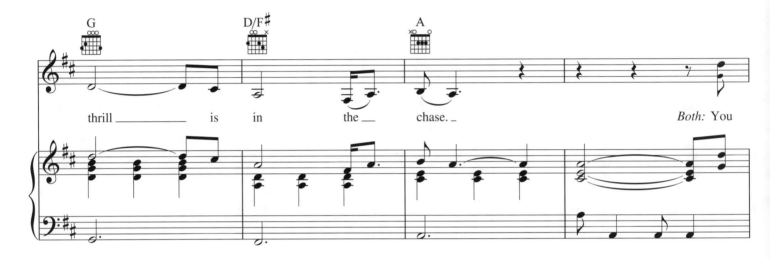

thrill _____ is in the _ chase. _ *Both:* You

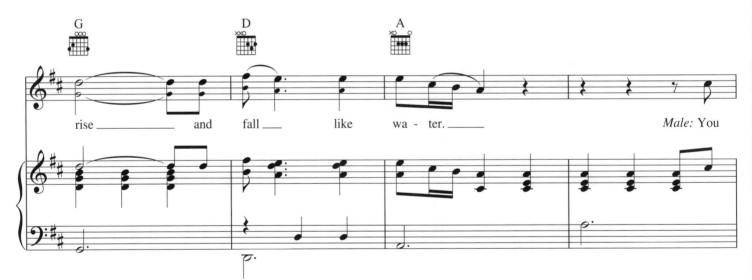

rise _____ and fall _ like wa - ter. _____ *Male:* You

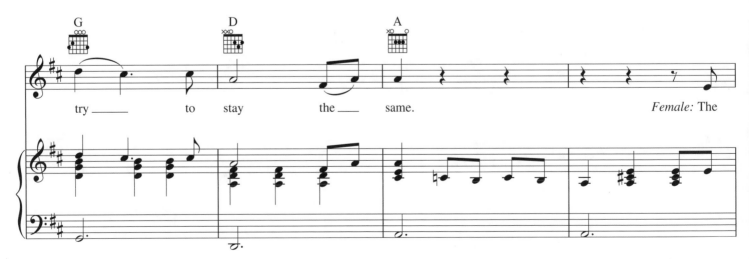

try _____ to stay the _ same. *Female:* The

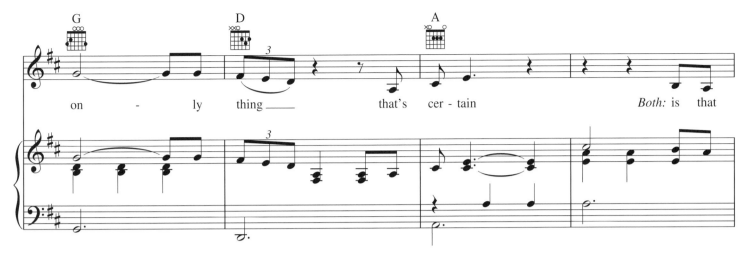

on - ly thing _____ that's cer - tain *Both:* is that

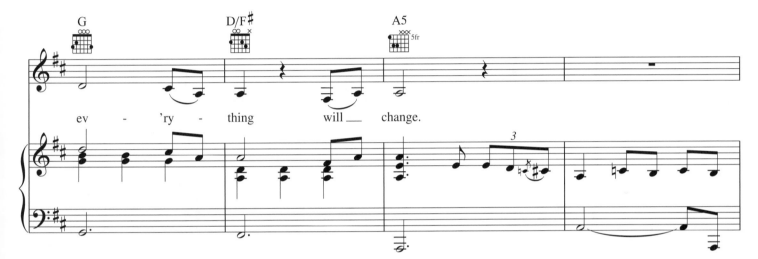

ev - 'ry - thing will _____ change.

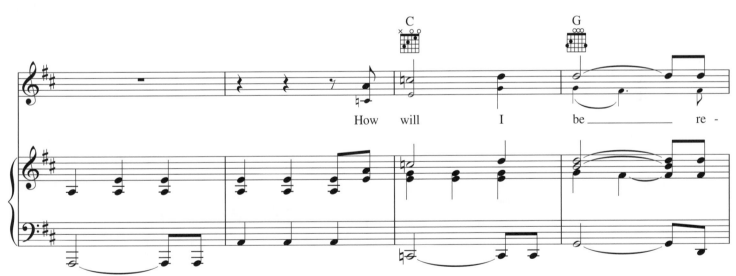

How will I be _____ re -

mem - bered? _____ *Male:* Will my crit - ics *Both:* be un -

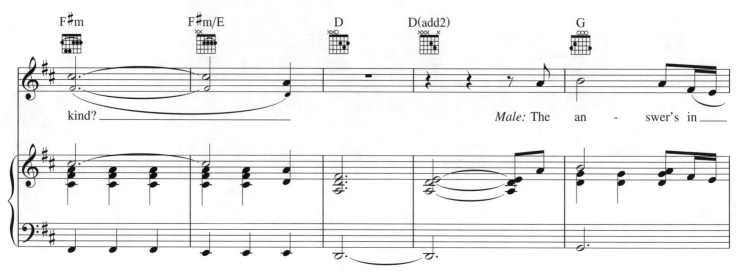

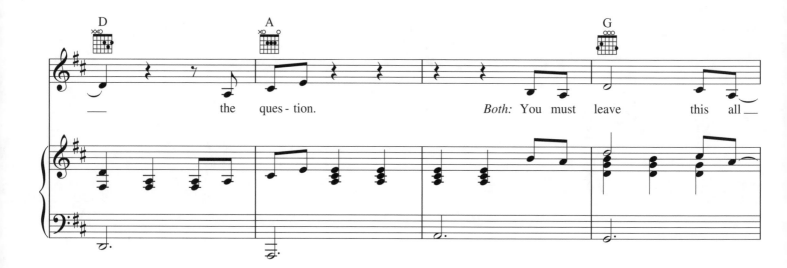

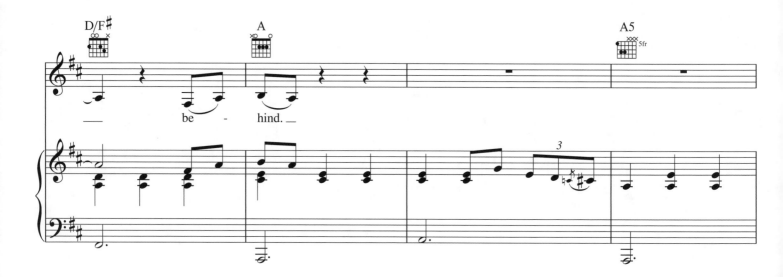

THE LONG GOODBYE

Words and Music by
BOB SEGER

Does it ___ chill or warm ___ your ___ soul to - night? ___
stay a - while or and then ___ you're ___ gone a - gain. ___

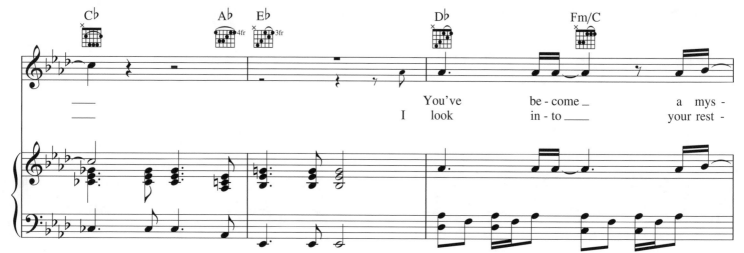

___ You've be - come ___ a mys -
___ I look in - to ___ your rest -

- ter - y. Will I earn your
- less eyes. You ___ turn a - way; it's

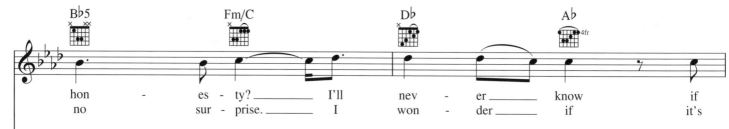

hon - es - ty? ___ I'll nev - er ___ know if
no sur - prise. ___ I won - der ___ if it's

To Coda

we a - gree if you're not
e - ven___ wise, but I'm still

here.   And we

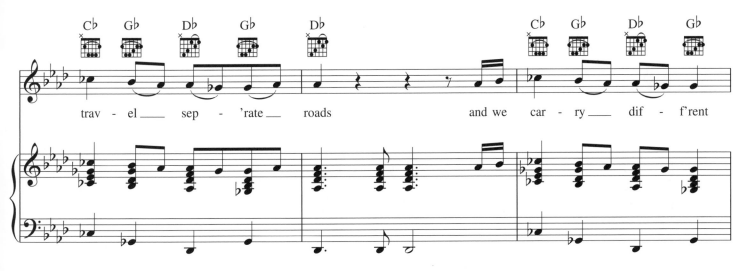

trav - el___ sep - 'rate___ roads   and we car - ry___ dif - f'rent

loads, __   and in the end we stay   or _____

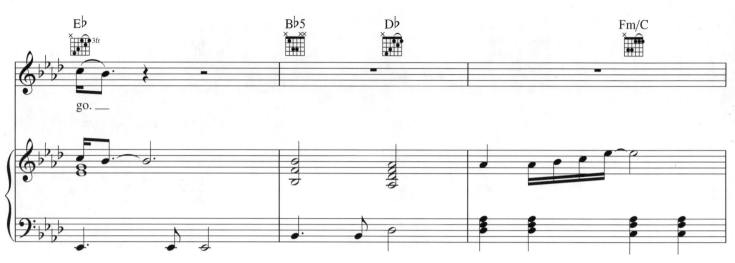

go.

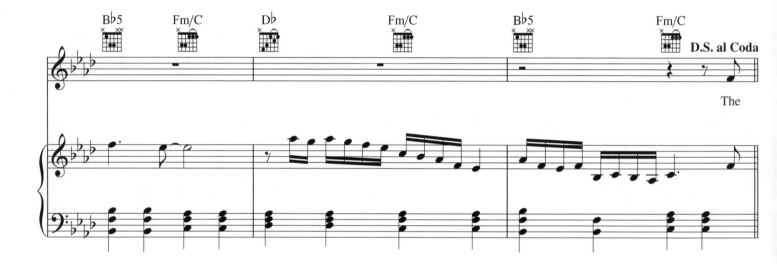

D.S. al Coda

The

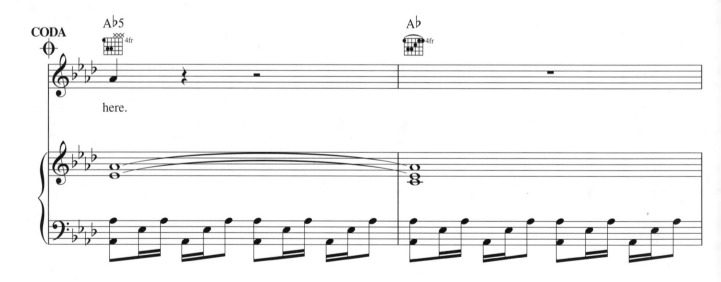

CODA

here.